I Am Wherever You Are

HELLO FROM HEAVEN

JENNIFER ECK

ILLUSTRATED BY
SETH AND LEANNE ECK

ISBN 978-1-63885-383-1 (Paperback)
ISBN 978-1-63885-385-5 (Hardcover)
ISBN 978-1-63885-384-8 (Digital)

Covenant Books
11661 Hwy 707
Murrells Inlet, SC 29576
www.covenantbooks.com

In loving memory of Jack Heintzelman and Patrick Eck. Your "hellos from heaven" have brightened our smiles and warmed our hearts. Thank you for always being wherever we are.

For my beautiful Earth angels—Brady, Charlotte, & Alexandra—PSALM 91:11. I love you! And for my love, my world: Jason, I Will Be Here—JLE

For Evelyn & Annabel—S&L

Someone I love went to heaven, but I know it's not the end. Now I always search for the beautiful signs my angel sends.

On the first day of school when I'm feeling nervous, I watch a butterfly while I walk to the bus.

A small but special reminder that you are near.
Even though you live in heaven, you are still here.

3

Time for dance class; I'm wearing my prettiest pink tutu.
I look down to see a white feather near my tap shoe.
A small but special reminder that you never miss a thing,
makes my face smile and my heart sing.

6

Sometimes I'm doing something boring like shopping at the store.
Even then, I find pennies and silver coins sparkling on the floor.
A small but special reminder that you are with me today
and always guiding me on my way.

I scored a goal at soccer, my favorite place to be.
As I celebrate, I spot a cardinal in a tree.
A small but special reminder that you are cheering me on.
Even though I cannot see you, you are not really gone.

The radio is on, and I'm rocking along.
Somehow the DJ always plays our song.
A small but special reminder that you still sing to me.
In my heart is your melody.

When I am driving around town or somewhere very far,
I love when I see the make and model of *your car*.
A small but special reminder that brings me such peace—
as I realize our bond will never cease.

The holidays have arrived, and we found the perfect tree.
Two eagles soar overhead in their majestic beauty.
A small but special reminder that you are here for it all—
Winter, spring, summer, or fall.

16

It's opening day for swim team, a sport that I love.
I notice a heart-shaped cloud above.
A small but special reminder from you to me.
Helps me remember that we are still we.

Sitting on the beach with sunshine on my face.
A rainbow appears above the sea—what a perfect place.
A small but special reminder that our connection
continues to grow.
I will always treasure heaven's *hello*!

OCEAN CITY
N. J.

These beautiful signs are gifts, you see.
Sent from heaven to earth just for me.
Small but special reminders that your love lives inside of me.
Wherever I am, you will always be.

About the Author

Jennifer Eck was an elementary school teacher prior to becoming a stay-at-home mother of three. After experiencing the crushing and untimely loss of her father, Jack, she found comfort in discovering "signs from heaven" in the form of butterflies, coins, hearts, feathers, and cars. Her  young children began to recognize these "hellos from Papa" in their daily lives, and they took great joy in sharing the special sightings with their family. Jennifer was inspired to write her first children's book with the genuine hope that it will provide comfort to all children who are experiencing the profound loss of a loved one. She shares her life with her husband and three children in New Jersey. Jen invites you to share your signs from heaven with her community on Instagram! Follow her page—IAWYA_hellofromheaven—and tag your photos: #iawya #hellofromheaven #signsfromheaven.

About the Illustrator

Seth and LeAnne Eck are a husband-and-wife team who collaborated to illustrate their first children's book. Seth, a high school art teacher, and LeAnne, a graphic designer, have two daughters who mean the world to them. Seth and LeAnne were honored when Jen asked them to illustrate her book in memory of Seth's father, Patrick. Together with their sister-in-law, they had a wonderful time creating a book that is so meaningful to their families.

CPSIA information can be obtained
at www.ICGtesting.com
Printed in the USA
BVHW022300290322
632819BV00014B/333